MORE
THAN
A JOB

Readings on Work and Society

▲▼▲

compiled by John Gordon

NEW READERS PRESS
Publishing Division of Laubach Literacy International
Syracuse, New York

PERMISSIONS FOR QUOTATIONS (pages 86-96)

From *The New Indians* by Stan Steiner. Copyright © 1968 by Stan Steiner. Reprinted by permission.

From *Working People Talk About What They Do All Day and How They Feel About What They Do* by Studs Terkel. Copyright © 1972, 1974 by Studs Terkel. Reprinted by permission of Pantheon Books, a division of Random House, Inc.

From *Illiterate America* by Jonathan Kozol. Copyright © 1986 by Doubleday & Co., a division of Bantam, Doubleday, Dell Publishing Group, Inc. Reprinted by permission.

From *Rereading America: Cultural Contexts for Critical Thinking and Writing* edited by Gary Colombo, Robert Cullen, and Bonnie Lisle. Copyright © 1989 by St. Martin's Press. Reprinted by permission.

From *My Life and Work* by Henry Ford. Copyright © 1926 by Doubleday & Co., a division of Bantam, Doubleday, Dell Publishing Group, Inc. Reprinted by permission.

From *Root & Branch: The Rise of the Workers' Movements* edited by Root and Branch. Reprinted by permission from Fawcett Publications.

From *Selected Writings in Sociology and Social Philosophy* by Karl Marx, compiled by Tom Bottomore. Copyright © 1964 by McGraw-Hill, Inc. Reprinted by permission.

ISBN 0-88336-859-5

Copyright © 1991
New Readers Press
Publishing Division of Laubach Literacy International
Box 131, Syracuse, New York 13210

All rights reserved. No part of this book may be reproduced or transmitted in any form or by any means, electronic or mechanical, including photocopying, recording, or by any information storage and retrieval system, without permission in writing from the publisher.

Printed in the United States of America

Illustration: Davis Henry
Cover Art: Stephen Rhodes
Design: Kathleen T. Bates
Production: Sharon Naftal

9 8 7 6 5 4 3 2

Contents

To the Reader • 5
John Gordon

Raymond's Run • 7
Toni Cade Bambara

Short-order Cook • 20
Jim Daniels

Waitresses • 22
Ranice Henderson Crosby

Uncle Claudio • 23
Nicholasa Mohr

As I Grew Older • 31
Langston Hughes

The Battle for Farmworkers' Rights • 33
Jessie Lopez de la Cruz
edited by Ellen Cantarow

Deferred • 74
Langston Hughes

Fast Car • 77
Tracy Chapman

Just a Housewife · 80
Jesusita Novarro
edited by Studs Terkel

Work and Dignity · 86
Quotations from various sources

Work, Status, and Recognition · 90
Quotations from various sources

To the Reader:

We all work. Some of us have paying jobs. Others stay at home—taking care of the children, getting them to school, cooking, doing the laundry, and taking care of the house. That's work, too, even though it's not always recognized. Whether we like it or not, work is a big part of our lives. In fact, most of us spend more time at work than at almost anything else we do.

It feels good to be able to go out and make money to support yourself and your family. Unfortunately, not everyone has that chance. A lot of people can't find a decent job. And for too many of us, work means standing in front of a machine all day long doing the same thing over and over. Too many of us spend our days getting told what to do by other people. Too often we know that our work doesn't contribute anything worthwhile to anybody. Too many of us are bored, unfulfilled, and underpaid.

We all know that there's a lot of work to be done. Many people are hungry. Many people don't have decent places to live or good health care. Why can't we find jobs if there are so many needs? Why can't we get work doing something we believe in? Why can't we get paid decently for what we do when there is so much wealth in the world?

Homelessness, unemployment, and poverty continue to grow. Meanwhile, on TV, in the newspapers, and in government, so-called experts debate what is to be done about these and other problems. These debates often shape our lives in ways we're not even aware of. But the voices of working people are not being heard. What do ordinary people think about their work, about the changes going on in the world? Who should work? How much should people be paid? Who should be in control of the workplace? What kinds of things should we be making and selling? These questions are too important to be left to the "experts."

This book is meant to draw you into those debates. Some of the writers in this book are famous; many are not. A lot of them are professional writers; others are not. Some are union organizers, welfare mothers, bank tellers, and steelworkers. Two were presidents; a few others were millionaires. Some were born in this century; others wrote a long time ago. But all of them speak with passion about people and their work.

You'll read the words of Jessie Lopez de la Cruz, a farmworker turned union organizer; of Langston Hughes, one of America's finest poets; of Smohalla, a Native American leader; and of many others.

I hope you enjoy reading this book. I hope it helps you to think about your own work and the role of work in all our lives. I hope you talk about it with your friends and your family. More than anything else, I hope it encourages you to raise your voice and speak out on the issues that you care about.

– J.G.

Raymond's Run

Toni Cade Bambara

I DON'T HAVE MUCH WORK TO DO AROUND THE house like some girls. My mother does that. And I don't have to earn my pocket money by hustling; George runs errands for the big boys and sells Christmas cards. And anything else that's got to get done, my father does. All I have to do in life is mind my brother Raymond, which is enough.

Sometimes I slip and say my little brother Raymond. But as any fool can see he's much bigger and he's older too. But a lot of people call him my little brother cause he needs looking after cause he's not quite right. And a lot of smart mouths got lots to say about that too, especially when George was minding him. But now, if anybody has anything to say to Raymond, anything to say about his big head, they have to come by me. And I

From Gorilla, My Love *by Toni Cade Bambara. Copyright © 1960, 1963, 1964, 1965, 1968, 1970, 1971, 1972 by Toni Cade Bambara. Reprinted by permission of Random House, Inc.*

don't play the dozens or believe in standing around with somebody in my face doing a lot of talking. I much rather just knock you down and take my chances even if I am a little girl with skinny arms and a squeaky voice, which is how I got the name Squeaky. And if things get too rough, I run. And as anybody can tell you, I'm the fastest thing on two feet.

There is no track meet that I don't win the first place medal. I use to win the twenty-yard dash when I was a little kid in kindergarten. Nowadays it's the fifty-yard dash. And tomorrow I'm subject to run the quarter-mile relay all by myself and come in first, second, and third. The big kids call me Mercury cause I'm the swiftest thing in the neighborhood. Everybody knows that—except two people who know better, my father and me.

He can beat me to Amsterdam Avenue with me having a two fire-hydrant headstart and him running with his hands in his pockets and whistling. But that's private information. Cause can you imagine some thirty-five-year-old man stuffing himself into PAL shorts to race little kids? So as far as everyone's concerned, I'm the fastest and that goes for Gretchen, too, who has put out the tale that she is going to win the first place medal this year. Ridiculous. In the second place, she's got short legs. In the third place, she's got freckles. In the first place, no one can beat me and that's all there is to it.

I'm standing on the corner admiring the weather and about to take a stroll down Broadway so I can practice my breathing exercises, and I've got Raymond walking on the inside close to the buildings cause he's subject to fits of fantasy and starts thinking he's a circus performer and that the curb is a tightrope strung high in the air. And sometimes after a rain, he likes to step down off his tightrope right into the gutter and slosh around getting his shoes and cuffs wet. Then I get hit when I get home. Or sometimes if you don't watch him, he'll dash across traffic to the island in the middle of Broadway and give the pigeons a fit. Then I have to go behind him apologizing to all the old people sitting around trying to get some sun and getting all upset with the pigeons fluttering around them, scattering their newspapers and upsetting the waxpaper lunches in their laps. So I keep Raymond on the inside of me, and he plays like he's driving a stage coach which is O.K. by me so long as he doesn't run me over or interrupt my breathing exercises, which I have to do on account of I'm serious about my running and don't care who knows it.

Now some people like to act like things come easy to them, won't let on that they practice. Not me. I'll high prance down 34th Street like a rodeo pony to keep my knees strong even if it does get my mother uptight so that she walks ahead like she's not with me, don't know me, is all by herself on a shopping trip, and I am somebody else's crazy child.

Now you take Cynthia Procter for instance. She's just the opposite. If there's a test tomorrow, she'll say something like, "Oh I guess I'll play handball this afternoon and watch television tonight," just to let you know she ain't thinking about the test. Or like last week when she won the spelling bee for the millionth time, "A good thing you got 'receive,' Squeaky, cause I would have got it wrong. I completely forgot about the spelling bee." And she'll clutch the lace on her blouse like it was a narrow escape. Oh, brother.

But of course when I pass her house on my early morning trots around the block, she is practicing the scales on the piano over and over and over and over. Then in music class, she always lets herself get bumped around so she falls accidently on purpose onto the piano stool and is so surprised to find herself sitting there, and so decides just for fun to try out the ole keys and what do you know—Chopin's waltzes just spring out of her fingertips and she's the most surprised thing in the world. A regular prodigy. I could kill people like that.

I stay up all night studying the words for the spelling bee. And you can see me anytime of day practicing running. I never walk if I can trot and shame on Raymond if he can't keep up. But of course he does, cause if he hangs back someone's liable to walk up to him and get smart, or take his allowance from him, or ask him where he got that great big pumpkin head. People are so stupid sometimes.

So I'm strolling down Broadway breathing out and breathing in on counts of seven, which is my lucky number, and here comes Gretchen and her sidekicks—Mary Louise who used to be a friend of mine when she first moved to Harlem from Baltimore and got beat up by everybody till I took up for her on account of her mother and my mother used to sing in the same choir when they were young girls, but people ain't grateful, so now she hangs out with the new girl Gretchen and talks about me like a dog; and Rosie who is as fat as I am skinny and has a big mouth where Raymond is concerned and is too stupid to know that there is not a big deal of difference between herself and Raymond and that she can't afford to throw stones. So they are steady coming up Broadway and I see right away that it's going to be one of those Dodge City scenes cause the street ain't that big and they're close to the buildings just as we are. First I think I'll step into the candy store and look over the new comics and let them pass. But that's chicken and I've got a reputation to consider. So then I think I'll just walk straight on through them or over them if necessary. But as they get to me, they slow down. I'm ready to fight, cause like I said I don't feature a whole lot of chitchat, I much prefer to just knock you down right from the jump and save everybody a lotta precious time.

"You signing up for the May Day races?" smiles Mary Louise, only it's not a smile at all.

A dumb question like that doesn't deserve an answer. Besides, there's just me and Gretchen standing there really, so no use wasting my breath talking to shadows.

"I don't think you're going to win this time," says Rosie, trying to signify with her hands on her hips all salty, completely forgetting that I have whupped her behind many times for less salt than that.

"I always win cause I'm the best," I say straight at Gretchen who is, as far as I'm concerned, the only one talking in this ventriloquist-dummy routine.

Gretchen smiles but it's not a smile and I'm thinking

that girls never really smile at each other because they don't know how and don't want to know how and there's probably no one to teach us how cause grown-up girls don't know either. Then they all look at Raymond who has just brought his mule team to a standstill. And they're about to see what trouble they can get into through him.

"What grade you in now, Raymond?"

"You got anything to say to my brother, you say it to me, Mary Louise Williams of Raggedy Town, Baltimore."

"What are you, his mother?" sasses Rosie.

"That's right, Fatso. And the next word out of anybody and I'll be their mother too." So they just stand there and Gretchen shifts from one leg to the other and so do they. Then Gretchen puts her hands on her hips and is about to say something with her freckle-face self but doesn't. Then she walks around me looking me up and down but keeps walking up Broadway, and her sidekicks follow her. So me and Raymond smile at each other and he says, "Gidyap" to his team and I continue with my breathing exercises, strolling down Broadway toward the icey man on 145th with not a care in the world cause I am Miss Quicksilver herself.

▲▼▲

I take my time getting to the park on May Day because the track meet is the last thing on the program. The biggest thing on the program is the May Pole dancing which I can do without, thank you, even if my mother thinks it's a shame I don't take part and act like a girl for a change. You'd think my mother'd be grateful not to have to make me a white organdy dress with a big satin sash and buy me new white baby-doll shoes that can't be taken out of the box till the big day. You'd think she'd be glad her daughter ain't out there prancing around a May Pole getting the new clothes all dirty and sweaty and trying to act like a fairy or a flower or whatever you're supposed to be when you should be trying to be yourself, whatever that is, which is, as far as I am concerned, a poor Black girl who really can't afford to buy shoes and a new dress you only wear once a lifetime cause it won't fit next year.

I was once a strawberry in a Hansel and Gretel pageant when I was in nursery school and didn't have no better sense than to dance on tiptoe with my arms in a circle over my head doing umbrella steps and being a perfect fool just so my mother and father could come dressed up and clap. You'd think they'd know better than to encourage that kind of nonsense. I am not a strawberry. I do not dance on my toes. I run. That is what I am all about. So I always come late to the May Day program, just in time to get my number pinned on and lay in the grass till they announce the fifty-yard dash.

I put Raymond in the little swings, which is a tight squeeze this year and will be impossible next year. Then I look around for Mr. Pearson who pins the numbers on. I'm really looking for Gretchen if you want to know the truth, but she's not around. The park is jam-packed. Parents in hats and corsages and breast-pocket handkerchiefs peeking up. Kids in white dresses and light blue suits. The parkees unfolding chairs and chasing the rowdy kids from Lenox as if they had no right to be there. The big guys with their caps on backwards, leaning against the fence swirling the basketballs on the tips of their fingers waiting for all these crazy people to clear out the park so they can play. Most of the kids in my class are carrying bass drums and glockenspiels and flutes. You'd think they'd put in a few bongos or something for real like that.

Then here comes Mr. Pearson with his clipboard and his cards and pencils and whistles and safety pins and fifty million other things he's always dropping all over the place with his clumsy self. He sticks out in a crowd cause he's on stilts. We used to call him Jack and the Beanstalk to get him mad. But I'm the only one that can outrun him and get away, and I'm too grown for that silliness now.

"Well, Squeaky," he says checking my name off the list and handing me number seven and two pins. And I'm thinking he's got no right to call me Squeaky, if I can't call him Beanstalk.

"Hazel Elizabeth Deborah Parker," I correct him and tell him to write it down on his board.

"Well, Hazel Elizabeth Deborah Parker, going to give someone else a break this year?" I squint at him real hard to see if he is seriously thinking I should lose the race on purpose just to give someone else a break.

"Only six girls running this time," he continues, shaking his head sadly like it's my fault all of New York didn't turn out in sneakers. "That new girl should give you a run for your money." He looks around the park for Gretchen like a periscope in a submarine movie. "Wouldn't it be a nice gesture if you were…to ahhh…"

I give him such a look he couldn't finish putting that idea into words. Grownups got a lot of nerve sometimes. I pin number seven to myself and stomp away—I'm so burnt. And I go straight for the track and stretch out on the grass while the band winds up with "Oh the Monkey Wrapped His Tail Around the Flag Pole," which my teacher calls by some other name. The man on the loudspeaker is calling everyone over to the track and I'm on my back looking at the sky trying to pretend I'm in the country, but I can't, because even grass in the city feels hard as sidewalk and there's just no pretending you are anywhere but in a "concrete jungle" as my grandfather says.

The twenty-yard dash takes all of the two minutes cause most of the little kids don't know no better than to run off the track or run the wrong way or run smack into the fence and fall down and cry. One little kid though has got the good sense to run straight for the white ribbon up ahead so he wins. Then the second graders line up for the thirty-yard dash and I don't even bother to turn my head to watch cause Raphael Perez always wins. He wins before he even begins by psyching the runners, telling them they're going to trip on their shoelaces and fall on their faces or lose their shorts or something, which he doesn't really have to do since he is very fast, almost as fast as I am. After that is the forty-yard dash which I use to run when I was in first grade. Raymond is hollering from the swings cause he knows I'm about to do my thing cause the man on the loudspeaker has just announced the fifty-yard dash, although he might just as well be giving a recipe for Angel Food cake cause you can hardly make out what he's saying for the static. I get up and slip off my sweat pants and then I see Gretchen standing at the starting line kicking her legs out like a pro. Then as I get into place I see that ole Raymond is in line on the other side of the fence, bending down with his fingers on the ground just like he knew what he was doing. I was going to yell at him but then I didn't. It burns up your energy to holler.

Every time just before I take off in a race, I always feel like I'm in a dream, the kind of dream you have when you're sick with fever and feel all hot and weightless. I dream I'm flying over a sandy beach in the early morning sun, kissing the leaves of the trees as I fly by. And there's always the smell of apples, just like in the country when I was little and use to think I was a choo-choo train, running through the fields of corn and chugging up the hill to the orchard. And all the time I'm dreaming this, I get lighter and lighter until I'm flying over the beach again, getting blown through the sky like a feather that weighs nothing at all. But once I spread my fingers in the dirt and crouch over for the Get on Your Mark, the dream goes and I am solid again and am telling myself, Squeaky you must win, you must win, you are the fastest thing in the world, you can even beat your father up Amsterdam if you really try. And then I feel my weight coming back just behind my knees then down to my feet then into the earth and the pistol shot explodes in my blood and I am off and weightless again, flying past the other runners, my arms pumping up and down and the whole world is quiet except for the crunch as I zoom over the gravel in the track. I glance to my left and there is no one. To the right a blurred Gretchen who's got her chin jutting out as if it would win the race all by itself. And on the other side of the fence is Raymond with his arms down to his side and the palms tucked up behind him, running in his very own style and the first time I ever saw that and I almost stop to watch my brother Raymond on his first run. But the white ribbon is bouncing toward me and I tear past it racing into the distance till my feet with a mind of their own start digging up footfuls of dirt and brake me short. Then all the kids standing on the side pile on me, banging me on the back and slapping my head with their May Day programs, for I have won again and everybody on 151st Street can walk tall for another year.

"In first place..." the man on the loudspeaker is clear as a bell now. But then he pauses and the loudspeaker starts to whine. Then static. And I lean down to catch my breath and here comes Gretchen walking back for she's overshot the finish line too, huffing and puffing with her hands on her hips taking it slow, breathing in steady time like a real pro and I sort of like her a little for the first time. "In first place..." and then three or four voices get all mixed up on the loudspeaker and I dig my sneaker into the grass and stare at Gretchen who's staring back, we both wondering just who did win. I can hear old Beanstalk arguing with the man on the loudspeaker and then a few others running their mouths about what the stop watches say.

Then I hear Raymond yanking at the fence to call me and I wave to shush him, but he keeps rattling the fence like a gorilla in a cage like in them gorilla movies, but then like a dancer or something he starts climbing up nice and easy but very fast. And it occurs to me, watching how smoothly he climbs hand over hand and remembering how he looked running with his arms down to his side and with the wind pulling his mouth back and his teeth showing and all, it occurred to me that Raymond would make a very fine runner. Doesn't he always keep up with me on my trots? And he surely knows how to breathe in counts of seven cause he's always doing it at the dinner table, which drives my brother George up the wall. And I'm smiling to beat the band cause if I've lost this race, or if me and Gretchen tied, or even if I've won, I can always retire as a runner and begin a whole new career as a coach with Raymond as my champion. After all, with a little more study I can beat Cynthia and her phony self at the spelling bee. And if I bugged my mother, I could get piano lessons and become a star. And I have a big rep as the baddest thing around. And I've got a roomful of ribbons and medals and awards. But what has Raymond got to call his own?

So I stand there with my new plan, laughing out loud by this time as Raymond jumps down from the fence and runs over with his teeth showing and his arms down to the side which no one before him has quite mastered as a running style. And by the time he comes over I'm jumping up and down so glad to see him—my brother Raymond, a great runner in the family tradition. But of course everyone thinks I'm jumping up and down because the men on the loudspeaker have finally gotten themselves together and compared notes and are announcing "In first place—Miss Hazel Elizabeth Deborah Parker." (Dig that.) "In second place—Miss Gretchen P. Lewis." And I look over at Gretchen wondering what the P stands for. And I smile. Cause she's good, no doubt about it. Maybe she'd like to help me coach Raymond; she obviously is serious about running, as any fool can see. And she nods to congratulate me and then she smiles. And I smile. We stand there with this big smile of respect between us. It's about as real a smile as girls can do for each other, considering we don't practice real smiling every day you know, cause maybe we too busy being flowers or fairies or strawberries instead of something honest and worthy of respect...you know...like being people.

Short-order Cook

Jim Daniels

An average joe comes in
and orders thirty cheeseburgers and thirty fries.

I wait for him to pay before I start cooking.
He pays.
He ain't no average joe.

The grill is just big enough for ten rows of three.
I slap the burgers down
throw two buckets of fries in the deep frier
and they pop pop spit spit...
psss...
The counter girls laugh.
I concentrate.
It is the crucial point—
they are ready for the cheese:
my fingers shake as I tear off slices
toss them on the burgers/fries done/dump/
refill buckets/burgers ready/flip into buns/
beat that melting cheese/wrap burgers in plastic/
into paper bags/fries done/dump/fill thirty bags/
bring them to the counter/wipe sweat on sleeve
and smile at the counter girls.

From Places Everyone *by Jim Daniels. Copyright © 1985 by University of Wisconsin Press. Reprinted by permission.*

I puff my chest out and bellow:
"Thirty cheeseburgers, thirty fries!"
They look at me funny.
I grab a handful of ice, toss it in my mouth
do a little dance and walk back to the grill.
Pressure, responsibility, success,
thirty cheeseburgers, thirty fries.

Waitresses

Ranice Henderson Crosby

I think they give us uniforms
so we remember who we are
that's what I think.

our faces are
one gigantic grin.
I don't think they even notice
when we show our teeth
and raise our hackles.
we're always smiling
and nodding
and pleasing.

as for me
my uniform feels like skin.

"Waitresses" by Ranice Henderson Crosby. Copyright © 1975 by Ranice Henderson Crosby. Reprinted by permission.

Uncle Claudio

Nicholasa Mohr

JAIME AND CHARLIE SAT ON THE STOOP WAITING for the rest of their family to come down. They were all going to the airport to see Uncle Claudio and Aunt Chela take the plane back to Puerto Rico.

Charlie had arrived in the Bronx very early this morning with his parents and older sisters. They had driven in from Manhattan. The two boys were first cousins. They saw each other only on special holidays and at family meetings, and today they were glad to be together again.

It was a warm spring Saturday morning. People were still in their apartments and the streets were empty. The boys sat silently, watching the traffic roll by and listening to the faraway sounds coming from inside the tenements. People were beginning to open their

---

From El Bronx Remembered *by Nicholasa Mohr. Copyright © 1985 by Arte Publico Press. Reprinted by permission.*

windows and turn on their radios. After a while, Jaime stood up and stretched.

"How about a game of stoop ball, Charlie?" he asked, smiling and holding up a Spalding ball.

"Better not," warned Charlie. "I got my good clothes on. You too, Jaime. We'll get it if we get dirty."

Bouncing the ball quickly against the stoop steps a few times, Jaime stopped and sighed. "You're right," he said.

"They sure are taking their sweet time coming down, ain't they?"

"True," answered Jaime, "but they gotta be at the airport at a certain time, so they can't be too late."

"Jaime, do you know why Uncle Claudio is going back to Puerto Rico so fast?" asked Charlie. "He only been here a few months. My mother and father were just talking this morning about how foolish he is to leave. Giving up a good job and good pay and all."

"My mother and father say the same thing like yours. But I know why he's going back to Puerto Rico."

"You do?"

"Yeah," answered Jaime, "I do."

"Tell me."

"Well, I came home from playing ball one day, I guess about a couple of weeks ago. As I came up the stairs I heard a noise, like someone crying. When I came to my floor, there was Uncle Claudio, standing in front of our door. He had his face buried in his hands and was crying out loud."

"Crying?" interrupted Charlie.

"Yes, he was. Because I tapped him and he turned around. His face was full of tears, and when he saw me he just took out his handkerchief, blew his nose, and went into our apartment real quick."

"Why was he crying?"

"I didn't know why, then. He went right into his room, and I forgot about it. But later that evening, I was doing my homework in my room and I heard a lotta noise coming from the kitchen. It sounded like a big argument so I went to see what was happening. Papi was standing and shouting at Uncle Claudio, and Aunt Chela was crying and wiping her eyes. My mother was trying to calm down my father."

"What were they saying?"

"Well, Papi was telling Uncle Claudio that he was an ungrateful brother to be going back to Humacao, after all he and Mami had done for him and Aunt Chela. You know, get them jobs and all. Well, all of a sudden Uncle Claudio jumped up, clenching his fists at Papi. You know what a bad temper my father has, so I thought, Uh-oh, here it comes; they are gonna stomp each other. But when Papi put up his hands to fight back, Uncle Claudio sat down and began to cry. Burst right out into tears just like in the hallway!" Jaime paused and nodded.

"Wow," said Charlie. "Did he tell why he was crying?"

"Wait, I'm coming to that. At first, everybody started asking him a whole lotta questions. He kept saying in Spanish, 'No puede ser,' something like that, you know, like 'It can't never be.' Like that. Then he started to tell why he can't stay here in this country. First, he says there are too many people all living together with no place to go. In his own home, in Humacao, people take it easy and know how to live. They got respect for each other, and know their place. At home, when he walks down the street, he is Don Claudio. But here, in New York City, he is Don Nobody, that's what he said. He doesn't get no respect here. Then he tells something that happened to him that day, in the subway, that he says made him make up his mind to go back home."

"What was that?"

"Well, he got on at his regular station downtown and there was no seats. So he stands, like always, and he notices two young men whispering to each other and pointing at him. At first he don't recognize them. But then one of them looks familiar. They are both well dressed, with suits and ties. One guy waves to him and smiles, so he waves back. Then the guy starts to call out to him by his first name. He says he is Carlito, the son of a lady called Piedad. She used to work for my father and Uncle Claudio's family back in Puerto Rico. The lady used to do the cleaning and cooking, and she was fired. Uncle Claudio says that this young guy is talking real loud and thanks him for firing his mother, because they came to this country and now are doing real well. He even told Uncle Claudio he has no bad feelings and offered him his seat. Then he asked Uncle Claudio where he worked and offered him a better job in his place. Well, Uncle Claudio said he was so embarrassed he got off before his stop, just to get away from that young guy."

"He did?" asked Charlie. "Why?"

"That's exactly what my Papi asked him. Why? Well, Uncle Claudio got real red in the face and started hollering at Papi. He said that in Humacao the maid's son would never talk to him like that. Here, that punk can wear a suit and tie while he has to wear dirty clothes all day. Back home in Humacao, Uncle Claudio says he could get that guy fired and make him apologize for the way he spoke to him, calling him by his first name like that. His mother was caught stealing food and was fired…and that she was lucky they did not put her in jail! Anyway, Papi tries to explain to him that things are different here. That people don't think like that, and that these things are not important. That there are better opportunities here in the future for Uncle Claudio's sons. And that Uncle Claudio has to be patient and learn the new ways here in this country." Jaime stopped talking for a moment.

"What did Uncle Claudio say?"

"He got really mad at Papi," said Jaime. "He says that Papi is losing all his values here in New York, and that he don't want his boys to come here, ever. That he is glad he left them in Humacao. There, they know that their father is somebody. He says he is ashamed of his younger brother—you know, my father. Anyway, everybody tried to calm him down and talk him out of going. Even Aunt Chela. I think she likes it here. But he got so excited he jumped up and made the sign of the cross and swore by Jesucristo and la Virgen María that he will never come back to El Bronx again! That was it, he made up his mind to go back, right there!"

"That was it?"

"Yes," Jaime nodded. "That's what happened."

"I don't know," said Charlie, shaking his head. "But I don't care who I meet on the subway, because I may never meet them again. I never see the same people on the subway twice even. Do you? Maybe Uncle Claudio didn't know that."

"You are right, but it wouldn't make no difference because he just made up his mind to leave."

"Anyway," Charlie said, "what's so bad about what that guy said? In fact I thought he seemed nice—giving him his seat and all. Maybe it was something else, and he's not saying the truth."

"No," Jaime said, "that was it. I know; I was there."

"Well, that's no big deal if you ask me. I thought it was something bad," Charlie said.

"I know," said Jaime, "and when I asked Papi why Uncle Claudio got so excited and has to leave, he said that Uncle Claudio lives in another time and that he is dreaming instead of facing life."

"What does that mean?" asked Charlie.

"I asked him the same thing. I don't know what that means neither. And Papi told me that when I grow up I'll understand. Then he started to laugh a whole lot and said that maybe I'll never understand."

"That's what your father said?"

"That's what he said. Nothing else," answered Jaime.

"Well..." Charlie shrugged his shoulders and looked at Jaime.

They sat silently for a while, enjoying the bright sun as it warmed their bodies and the stone steps of the stoop.

Very young children played, some on the sidewalk, others in the street. They chalked areas for different games, forming groups. The men were lining up in front of their parked cars with buckets of water, detergent, car wax, and tool boxes. They called out to one another as they began the long and tedious ritual of washing, polishing and fixing their secondhand automobiles.

Windows opened; some of the women shook out the bedclothes, others leaned against the mattresses placed on the sills for an airing and looked out along the avenue. The streets were no longer empty. People hustled and bustled back and forth, and the avenue vibrated with activity.

Jaime and Charlie grew restless.

"Too bad we can't go over to the schoolyard and play ball," said Jaime.

"Here they come at last!" said Charlie.

Uncle Claudio walked by with his wife, Chela. The boys noticed that he wore the same outfit he had arrived with last year: a white suit, white shirt with a pale-blue tie, white shoes, and a very pale beige, wide-brimmed, panama hat. Aunt Chela had a brand-new dress and hat.

The adults talked among themselves as they decided how to group the families into the two cars.

"We wanna ride together, Papi. Please, me and Charlie!" Jaime pulled his father's arm.

"O.K.," said his father, "you two jump in." He pointed to one of the cars.

Jaime and Charlie sat together, enjoying the ride.

"What do you think? If we get back in time, how about going to the schoolyard and have a game of stickball? You can meet all my friends," said Jaime.

"Right!" answered Charlie.

As I Grew Older

Langston Hughes

It was a long time ago.
I have almost forgotten my dream.
But it was there then,
In front of me,
Bright like a sun—
My dream.

And then the wall rose,
Rose slowly,
Slowly,
Between me and my dream.
Rose slowly, slowly,
Dimming,
Hiding,
The light of my dream.
Rose until it touched the sky—
The wall.

Shadow.
I am black.

From Selected Poems of Langston Hughes *by Langston Hughes. Copyright © 1926 by Alfred A. Knopf, Inc. and renewed 1954 by Langston Hughes. Reprinted by permission.*

I lie down in the shadow.
No longer the light of my dream before me,
Above me.
Only the thick wall.
Only the shadow.

My hands!
My dark hands!
Break through the wall!
Find my dream!
Help me to shatter this darkness,
To smash this night,
To break this shadow
Into a thousand lights of sun,
Into a thousand whirling dreams
Of sun!

The Battle for Farmworkers' Rights

Jessie Lopez de la Cruz
edited by Ellen Cantarow

Rootedness and Uprooting

MY GRANDMOTHER WAS BORN IN MEXICO IN AGUAS Calientes, near Guadalajara. She was raised by a very strict father and she married at thirteen. That was the custom. The girls, as soon as they were old enough to learn cooking and sewing, would get married. Most married at twelve or thirteen. My grandmother married and she was left out in a little shack by herself. She was so young, so afraid...

She had my mother and my oldest brother when she and my grandfather came across.[1] My grandfather

From Moving the Mountain: Women Working for Social Change, edited by Ellen Cantarow with Susan Gushee O'Malley and Sharon Hartman Strom. Copyright © 1980 by Ellen Cantarow. Published by The Feminist Press at CUNY. Reprinted by permission.

worked for the railroad laying the ties and tracks. Then he worked for a mining company. After that we moved to Anaheim. We lived in a big four-bedroom house my grandfather built. With my grandparents and their children, three children of my mother's sister who had died, and the three of us, that made a big crowd.

My grandfather would get up Sunday mornings and start the fire in a great big wood-burning stove. He would wrap us up in blankets and seat us around that stove on chairs and say, "Now, don't get too close to the stove. Take care of the younger children." Then he would go out to the store and get bananas and oranges and cereal that he'd cook for us to eat, and milk, and he would feed us Sunday mornings.

My grandmother had a beautiful garden—carnations and pansies and roses, and a big bush of bleeding heart. She was very proud of that. My grandfather used to grow a vegetable garden in back of our house; we had a large yard. And I remember that while he was working for the company, he got us one of those big cement pipes with a hole in the bottom. He would plug that up with a piece of wood he carved to fit the hole, and then he would fill this up with water. My brothers and I would get into it. We had a grand time with that!

But then, I remember, there was a flood one night. We were all scared, and we were crying because it was raining very hard and water and oil from some oil wells around there were just running down the streets into homes. There was oil all over, inside the house. My grandfather and the older children and neighbors had lanterns and shovels, and they were piling up mud to keep the water from going into our houses. We were taken to the second floor of a store. Many families spent the night there. The next day, when we went home, my grandmother cried because her flowers were all gone—full of oil and mud.

Then my grandfather had an accident. The middle finger of his right hand was crushed, and he couldn't work for about two weeks. When he went back he was told that he'd already been replaced by another worker. So he was out of a job. He decided we'd better go on and pick the crops. We had done that before, during the summer. But this time we went for good.

We came north. The families got together; the women would start cooking at night, boiling eggs and potatoes and making piles of tortillas and tacos, and these lunches would be packed in pails and boxes. There was as much fruit as they could get together, and roasted pumpkin seeds. My uncle had a factory where he made Mexican candy in East Los Angeles. And he used to give us a lot of pumpkin seeds. So my mother dried these, and she roasted and salted them for the trip to keep the drivers awake. We'd start in a car caravan, six or seven families together, one car watching for the other, and when it got a little dark they'd pull onto the roadside and build a fire and start some cooking to feed us. Then they'd spread blankets and quilts on the ground, and we would sleep there that night. The next morning, the women and older children would get up first and start the breakfast. And we smaller children, it was our job to fold the blankets and put them back in the cars and trucks. Then my brothers and the men would check the cars over again, and after breakfast all the women would wash the dishes and pack them, get 'em in the cars, and we'd start again.

We'd finally get to Delano and we would work there a little.[2] If work was scarce, we would keep on going till San José. I did the same thing my mother and my grandfather and my uncles did, picking prunes on our hands and knees off the ground, and putting them in the buckets. We were paid four dollars a ton, and we had to fill forty boxes to make it a ton. They made us sign a contract that we would stay there until all the prunes were picked. When we would finish the prunes, in early September, we would start back. And stop on the way to Mendota to pick cotton.

When I was about thirteen, I used to lift a twelve-foot sack of cotton with 104 or 112 pounds. When you're doing this work, you get to be an expert. I could get that sack and put it on my shoulder, and walk with that sack for about a city block or maybe a little less, to where the scale was. I could hook this sack up on the scale, have it weighed, take it off the hook, and put it back on my shoulder; and walk up a ladder about eight-feet high and dump all that cotton in the trailer.

My brothers taught me how to do it. When I first started picking cotton, they had to untie their sack and go on my side of the row and help me put this sack on my shoulder, so they taught me how to do it when it was full. It's stiff. My brother said, "Just walk over it, pick up one end, and sort of pull it up, up, and then bend, and when the middle of the sack hits your shoulder, you just stand up slowly. Then put your arm on your waist, and the sack will sit on your shoulder and you can just walk with it." At thirteen, fourteen, I was lifting 104 and 112 pounds. I weighed ninety-five, I guess!

As a child, I remember we had tents without any floors. It was Giffen's Camp Number Nine. I remember the water coming from under the tent at night to where we were sleeping. My brothers would get up with shovels and put mud around the tent to keep the water out. But our blankets and our clothes were always damp during the winter.

There were truckloads that got brought in, of little blocks of wood from some lumber company. People could go out and get some of those for heating or for cooking in those oil drums or woodburning stoves, if they happened to have one. We had an oil drum. There were too many people and not enough wood to go around, so my brothers would have to go out and hunt for something to burn in the stove so we could cook.

There was a lot of disease. I don't remember two weeks out of my life: I had typhoid fever. I was put in the hospital in Bakersfield. At that time, we lived in some kind of tin building where they stored grain and apricot after it's been dried, and raisins. During the winter, I recall, I'd get up in the morning and want to wash my hands and face. We had to run quite a distance to the water faucet. I'd open the faucet and no water would come out: it was frozen. There was a barrel underneath with just a block of ice on the top. I would break this with my hands and wash my face and hands in a hurry and run back to the house and get ready for school. And in this water you'd see little things crawling up and going down. I don't know what they're called. But the typhoid is from water that's standing too long in one place, like this barrel, where my brothers and sisters and the other kids washed.

At Di Giorgio, another big camp, one of the big growers that the United Farmworkers were fighting for a time, my little sister was burned to death in a fire, an accident. It was 1929, and then in 1930 my mother died: I think she had cancer but we don't know. I remember waking at night and hearing her cry, just in pain, you know. I'd start crying under the blankets, and my grandmother would come and say, "No, don't cry, just be quiet, your mama's gonna be all right." My grandmother would get water as hot as she could and dip towels in it and put it on my mother's back where she had this pain. My grandmother took my mother to the county hospital, and when she got back I didn't recognize my mother. Her hair had been cut short above her ears and she was thin; her eyes were sunken; I just didn't know her. I was crying all the time. She finally died in March: I wasn't ten yet. And then in June my grandfather died—same year. It was very hard for my grandmother. She had seven children. And then my sister and myself made it nine.

We had some very hard times. In 1930, a friend of my grandmother gave her some money. She got some *menudos* (tripe) and hominy. She said, "Take out those pots and soak this." She soaked the tripe, added garlic. The next day, she got my brother to go with her with a little cart. She went from house to house selling *menudo*. The money she raised from that, she'd buy more. She'd use what was left over to feed us. There was no wood for heating. And one time, to top it off, we all got scarlet fever: they put a sign on our door. Nobody was to go in or out.

We'd go out on the hilltop and pick mushrooms, mustard greens. My brothers would kill wild rabbits. And this we would eat during the winter.

In '33, we came up north to follow the crops because my brothers couldn't find any work in Los Angeles during the Depression. I remember going hungry to school. I didn't have a sweater. I had nothing. I'd come to school and they'd want to know, "What did you have for breakfast?" They gave us a paper, to write down what we had! I *invented* things! We had eggs and milk, I'd say, and the same things the other kids would write, I'd write. There weren't many Mexican people at school, mostly whites, and I'd watch to see what they were writing or the pictures that they'd show. You know: glasses of milk, and toast, and oranges and bananas and cereal. I'd never had *anything*. My grandmother couldn't work, we couldn't work, so we went hungry. One of my friends at school said, "Jessie, why don't you eat with us?" And I said, "I don't have any money." So they talked to the teacher, and the teacher called me one day during recess. She said, "Jessie, where's your father?"

"I don't have one."

"Where's your mother?"

"I don't have one." Then she wanted to know who did I live with. I said my grandmother and my uncles and aunts. She said, "Did you eat any breakfast?"

"No."

"Did your brothers and sisters eat breakfast?"

"No."

"Did you bring a lunch?"

"No." So she said, "Well, you help us in the kitchen. You can help us clear the tables after all the children eat, and you and your brothers and sisters can come and eat." It got to where after school, everything that was left in those big pots they'd put in those gallon cans for tomato sauce or canned peaches, and say, "You can take these home with you." And I'd take them home and we'd have a party—my grandmother and everybody.

From there we moved again, this time to Dohenny Park, which is by the sea by San Juan Capistrano near Clemente. Sundays my grandmother would take us for walks. She'd take my sisters and some of our girlfriends, and we'd go hiking up those mountains and see all sorts of flowers and cactuses. We'd pick up all these wildflowers and just run out in the fields. Oh! I loved that.

We weren't feeling sorry for ourselves: we didn't know there was anything better than what we had. Everybody that came into the camp and stayed there lived the way we did. In the summer of 1934, this family came in and they had a radio. Boy! We had to make friends with those girls! One Sunday these girls came over to my house and asked if I could get my grandmother to let me go over to their house. I asked her. She said, "What do you want to visit them for?"

"Well, it's Julia and her sister and these other girls, they want me to go, and they were asking me. Would you let me?"

"Okay. But I'll be outside watching. Are there any boys there?"

"No, just girls. They have a radio and we want to listen to it." So we got this radio into an empty cabin where nobody lived. There were seven or eight girls and we danced with that radio. I guess our parents thought we should have a little fun because my brother came in one night and said, "Guess who's here? Doña Petra Moreno." She was from back home when my grandfather and my mother were living. We met them that night. Doña Petra Moreno had three boys, and they were musicians. One played the guitar, another the violin, and one played the banjo. It got to where during the summer we would string up lights around these empty cabins and the boys would play and the families would dance—the teenagers and the parents and everybody! Then we were having a good time!

Notes

1 Jessie De La Cruz calls her uncles "brothers." After the age of ten, she was raised by her grandmother, and some of her mother's brothers weren't much older than she was.

2 Delano is northeast of Los Angeles near the bottom of the San Joaquin Valley. It was in Delano that the great grape strike called by Cesar Chavez's National Farmworkers' Association, together with Larry Itliong's United Farmworkers' Organizing Committee, began in 1965.

Courtship, Marriage, and Childrearing

WHEN I WAS A GIRL, BOYS WERE ALLOWED TO GO out and have friends and visit there in the camp, and even go to town. But the girls—the mother was always watching them. We couldn't talk to nobody. If I had a boyfriend, he had to send me letters, drop notes on his way or send them along with somebody. We did no dating. We weren't allowed to. If girls came to visit at my house, my grandmother sat right there to listen to what we were talking about. We weren't allowed to speak English because she couldn't understand, and she would say, "How can I tell if you're talking about me or if you're fighting or something?" This is what I mean by sheltered. We were allowed nowhere except out to the field, and then we always worked between my two older brothers. One brother was on one side, and me next, then my two sisters, and then my next oldest brother on the other end. And we were not allowed to talk. The only one they trusted was Arnold. He's the one I married. He was allowed to come in our house any time of day. He was always joking and talking with my grandmother. Nights, he would come in and sit on the floor with us. I'd always have some songbooks, and he'd pick one up and look at it, and take out a pencil and start writing. He was writing me a note, and then he'd close the book and say, "Have you learned this song?" And he'd open the book for me to read and I'd read the note right in front of my grandmother! So now I understand the saying, where there is a will there's a way.

I was fourteen when I met Arnold, in 1933. We lived next door to his family, which was a big one. I'd go there and help Arnold's mother make stacks of tortillas. She didn't have time enough to do all the work for the little children. I'd go and help her. When she went to the hospital in 1935, when Arnold's younger brother was born, I cared for the whole family. I'd make tortillas and cook. The little ones we kept in our house, and the rest of them stayed in their cabin.

Arnold and I got married in 1938 in Firebaugh, where we'd all moved. We had a big party with an orchestra: some of Arnold's friends played the violin and guitar. But we had no honeymoon. On the second day after our wedding, he went back to his job—irrigating. I'd get up at four o'clock in the morning to fix his breakfast and his lunch. He'd start the fire for me. I did the cooking in his mother's kitchen. We had three cabins in all by this time. His mother had one cabin that was used as a bedroom. There was ours. And the other cabin in front was used as the kitchen for all of us. So in the morning I'd get up and run across and I'd fix his breakfast and his lunch and he'd go off and I'd go back to bed. He'd come home about four or five o'clock and there would be ice around his ears. It didn't come from the irrigating. It came from riding in the pickup. They were going fast, and the wind was that cold! He'd come home and get next to the stove where the fire was burning and have something hot to eat. He worked twelve hours a day.

I felt I was overworked in the house. I felt like saying, "Okay, there's the whole thing, you take care of it," but I couldn't. I felt, "What can Arnold's mother do without the help I'm giving her?" I felt sorry for her. She'd worked very hard and she had so many children, and had to wash her clothes in a tub with a rock board and do the ironing by heating the irons on top of the stove. All of us had to do this, but not many families had eight or nine little children.

I cooked with her until May. But I kept after Arnold: "I want my own kitchen!" So in May we drove all the way into Fresno. We got a few spoons and plates and pots and skillets, and I started my own housekeeping. I still went to his mother's to help her during the day when Arnold was working. But I cooked in my own stove.

After I was married, sometime in May, my husband was chopping cotton and I said, "I want to go with you."

"You can't! You have to stay at home!"

"I just feel like going outside somewhere. I haven't gone anyplace. I want to at least go out to the fields. Take another hoe and I'll help you." I went, but only for one or two days. Then he refused to take me. He said, "You have to stay home and raise children." I was pregnant with my first one. "I want you to rest," he said. "You're not supposed to work. You worked ever since I can remember. Now that you're married, you are going to rest." So I stayed home, but I didn't call it rest doing all the cooking for his mother.

Arnold was raised in the old Mexican custom—men on the one side, women on the other. Women couldn't do anything. Your husband would say, "Go here," you'd do it. You didn't dare go out without your husband saying you could.

Arnold never beat me, or anything like that. But every time I used to talk to him he didn't answer, even if I asked a question. He'd say, "Well, you don't have to know about it." If I asked, "Arnold, has the truck been paid for?" he wouldn't answer. Or I would ask him, "Did you pay the loan company?" he wouldn't answer. Then I'd get kind of mad and say, "Why can't you tell me?" and he'd say, "What do you want to know about it, are you going to pay for it, or what? Let me do the worrying." Now that is all changed; we talk things over. But in the beginning it was different.

The first year we were married, he was home every night. After the first year was up, I guess that was the end of the honeymoon. He would just take off, and I wouldn't see him for three or four days, even more. I didn't even ask, "Where were you?" I accepted it. I wasn't supposed to question him. He would come in and take his dirty clothes off, pile them up, and when I did the wash the next day I'd look through his pockets and find bus ticket stubs of where he'd been to—Santa Maria, miles and miles away from home. He would be home for about two days and then take off again with his friends, his pals who were gambling. I really couldn't blame him that much, because when he was young, before we were married, he was never even allowed to go to a dance. So he was trying out his wings.

After a time I said, "I have really had it. Why do you have to go with your friends all the time when I'm being left alone?"

"Well, what's wrong with that? You can go visit my mother." I said, "Big deal, you want me to go visit your mother and help make some tortillas." So he finally started giving me money, five or six dollars. He'd say, "My mother's going to Fresno. If you want to go with them you can go." Or he would say, "Doña Genoveva," a friend of ours, "is going to Fresno and she said you can come along." I'd get my kids—I had two of them—ready early in the morning and we'd go to Fresno or to visit her husband, who was up in the mountains in the hospital for TB. One day I just said, "Why do I have to depend on other people to take me out somewhere? I'm married, I have a husband—who should be taking me out." The next time he was home and said, "Here's the money," I said, "I don't want to go." He let it go at that, and I did, too. I didn't say another word. The following weekend he said, "Do you want to go to a show? My mother's going. They're going to Fresno." I said, "No." Then about the third time this happened he said, "Why don't you want to go anymore?"

"I do, I do want to go. I want to go somewhere, but not with anyone else. I want to go with you." So then he started staying home and he'd say, "Get ready, we're going into Fresno." And both of us would come in, bring the children, go to a show and eat, or just go to the park.

We'd come in about once a month and bring the children with us. They just loved that, and now they're always talking about it, how Arnold would sing funny songs for them all the way from camp to town, and we'd all have a good time. This began happening around 1942, when I was in my twenties.

Arnold would never teach me how to drive. One day I asked him to. We were on a ditch bank about eight-feet wide. He says, "Get on the driver's side. Now, turn around and go back." I got out. I said, "*You* do it! Just tell me you don't want me to learn if that's what you want." Then in 1947 I asked my sister, Margaret, and she showed me. We practiced in a field. After a few times she said, "Hey! You know how to drive! Let's go into town so you can buy your groceries."

So one day I said to Arnold, "I'm going out to get the groceries."

"Who's going to take you?"

"Me. Maggie taught me how to drive and it's about time I learned. I stay home and cook for all these men"—I was cooking in a boarding house in the camp at the time—"and if I run short I have to send for someone to go get it, and they never give me back my change. So I'm going to do the buying from now on."

Before I was married, in 1933, we would come and camp by the river in that place where we were picking grapes. After I was married, we still kept on coming there to pick grapes. We would get a blanket and tie it to the limbs of one of the trees, and to the chicken wire fence that divided the horses and cows and rabbits from us. We would sleep under this tree and do our cooking there and fight the flies. For walls, we used what they called sweat boxes. They're about the size of a three-by-five table. After the grapes are dried out in rows, they're picked up and put into sweat boxes. I would nail some of these together as a wall for privacy. Some I would place on the ground and put our mattress on top for a bed. By turning two boxes right side down, and a third on top right side up, I would fill the top one with dirt and put three rocks in a triangle. That would be our stove, where I would cook our meals.

Sometimes there were about twenty families camped the whole stretch of the riverbank. I'd do my washing there. If there was a big rock, we would scrub our clothes there. I'd get a tub and I'd put some water in it, and then I'd put the soap in there and I'd scrub the soap on the shirts or whatever, and I'd scrub on the rub board. When I first started, at around twelve, I got blisters on my knuckles, but later my grandmother taught me how to use the scrub board, and after that it was easy.

Of course I didn't wash sheets. We didn't have them. Pillowcases we didn't have. We just had the blankets, which I'd made out of flour sacks made of cotton. When I found out that I was pregnant with my first child, I didn't have anything to make clothes for him, so out of old shirts or flour sacks or whatever little pieces of material I could get, I used to make clothes I knew he was going to need. Then the next one came. Friends, after their babies had outgrown these clothes, they would give them to me, and then I'd pass them on to a neighbor that was having a baby. We always tried to help each other.

My first child was born in 1939, Ray. I had five more. I also took Susan, the girl my sister left when she died. Now I have fourteen grandchildren, and this spring it will be fifteen, sometime in May.

I stopped working toward the last months of my pregnancies, but I would start again after they were born. When I was working and I couldn't find somebody, I would take them with me. I started taking Ray with me when he wasn't a year old yet. I'd carry one of those big washtubs and put it under the vine and sit him there. I knew he was safe; he couldn't climb out. Arnold and I would move the tub along with us as we worked. I hated to leave him with somebody that probably wouldn't take care of him the way I could.

Once there was nearly an accident with Susan. It was when we were picking cotton. You know, you're picking the cotton and putting it in the sack, which is tied around your waist. When it got kind of full I used to put Susan right in the back and pull her along with my cotton. But then she got sleepy—she was a little over a year when we were picking cotton. I would get her blanket and put it ahead on the row—almost way out there by the end—lay her down and give her her bottle, and by the time we got finished picking up to where she was, then it would be time to go home. So one time I left her; I felt I wasn't too far away. I could hear her if she cried; it was silent although people were working. Then I saw this truck coming. It had a trailer hitched to it—not on the road where it was supposed to be, but on top of the cotton rows. My cotton sack was too full for me to lift up and run with it! There were about seventy-five pounds of cotton in there. I tried to untie it, but instead I made a knot in it, I was that nervous, yelling and crying! Arnold was trying to untie his sack, too. I called to one friend, kept shouting to the man in the truck to stop. By the time I got loose from the sack and got out there the truck had almost run over her. I said, "Never again will I put her out there!"

In 1944 we moved to a labor camp in Huron and we stayed there till 1956. But before that we had a single-room cabin. I used to separate the bed section from the kitchen by nailing blankets or pieces of canvas to divide. We had our bed and another bed for the children. All the boys slept in the bed, and the girl slept with us in our bed. During the night, Bobby being the youngest of the boys would wake up and be scared, and he always ended up in our bed! It was pretty crowded, but what could you do? I was always nailing orange crates on the walls to use as cupboards for dishes. Then I had a man build a cupboard for me. It had four shelves and a screen door to keep the flies out. The dishes I didn't use every day I kept there. Like if I happened to buy a cake plate, you know, those big ones with the long stem, I'd put it in there. I never had a set of dishes. I'd get pretty teacups I didn't want to use every day and put them in that cupboard. The rest went into those boxes.

Once, I remember, it was wintertime. We were so crowded, and I couldn't send the kids out to play. Night after night I kept saying, "You better go to sleep. It's late." But they'd be jumping up and down on the bed, which was on one side of my cupboard. I'd say, "Go to sleep. You're going to break my dishes." They'd be quiet for a little while, and start all over again. It finally happened. One day they knocked my cupboard over and broke all my dishes. I sat down and cried. I couldn't help it. I sat down on top of all that broken glass and said, "I'm going to run away. You won't mind me, you just won't do things when I ask you. You broke all my dishes. You'll never see me again! I'm going to run away!" They all started crying and hugging me. "Mama! Don't go!" Then I felt bad. How could I do this to them? "No," I said, "I'm not going to run away. But you have to mind me." They still remember that.

There was a lot of sickness. I remember when my kids got whooping cough. Arnold would come back late in the evening and wet, and the children were coughing and coughing. Arnold was sick, too, he was burning hot. During this time instead of staying in my own cabin at night I'd go to my mother-in-law's. The children would wake up at night coughing and there was blood coming out of their noses. I cried and cried, I was afraid they'd choke. I went to the clinic and they told me the children had whooping cough. That cough lasted six months.

I had a little girl who died in '43. She was so tiny... only five months. The cause was the way we were living, under the tree, with only chicken wire to separate us from the cows and horses. There were thousands of flies. I didn't have a refrigerator, no place to refrigerate the milk. She got sick. I couldn't stop the diarrhea. They told me she had a brain infection. And so I had to leave her, and my little girl died. We were so poor and I felt so helpless—there was nothing I could do.

It was like that for all of us. I would see babies who died. It was claimed if you lifted a young baby up fast, the soft spot would cave in and it would get diarrhea and dehydrate and die. After all these years I know it wasn't that that killed them. It was hunger, malnutrition, no money to pay the doctors. When the union came, this was one of the things we fought against.

Work in the Fields

FROM 1939 UNTIL 1944, WE STAYED AT GIFFEN'S Camp Number Three. We were still following the crops. We would go out to pick cotton or apricots or grapes here near Fresno, or we would go farther north to Tracey to pick peas. When there was no work chopping or picking cotton, we'd go to Patterson or San José to pick apricots. Arnold did the picking and I did cutting for the drying-out in the sheds. The apricots would be picked out in the field or in the orchard. They'd bring 'em in, in trucks, and they'd just set them beside us. They always had a boy or two that would dump these apricots on a table. We would have a knife, and we'd cut around it and take out the pit, and just spread them out on top of big trays. After we filled all these trays, they would come and take these out where they were dried. And they'd put some more on the table on the trays for us to cut.

We always went where the women and men were going to work, because if it were just the men working it wasn't worth going out there because we wouldn't earn enough to support a family. In one camp we were living at, the camp was at the edge of a cotton patch and the cotton needed to be thinned. We would start early. It was May. It got so hot, we would start around 6:30 A.M. and work for four or five hours, then walk home and eat and rest until about three-thirty in the afternoon when it cooled off. We would go back and work until we couldn't see. Then we'd get home and rest, visit, talk. Then I'd clean up the kitchen. I was doing the housework and working out in the fields and taking care of the kids. I had two children by this time.

Other times we would pick grapes. The sand is very hot. It gets up to about a hundred-eight, a hundred-ten degrees during the summer out in the fields. We wore tennis shoes to protect our feet from the hot sand. I'd get a pan and put it under the vine and cut the grapes. The grower wanted us to cut them, not pull them. You had to hold the grape bunches gently—not to crush the grapes—in your hand, and you'd have to use your knife to cut off from the stem and place the grapes in a pan. After that pan was full, you would spread these grapes in a paper tray where the sun was shining. But I was using my knife this way, and kept on cutting and cutting toward me, and these knives have a hook on them, and the handle is kind of rounded. One day I came to a real hard one. The stem was drying so I had to use a lot of strength, and this knife gave me a big cut on my neck. It scared me! Arnold said to just sit down and stay there. He washed the blood off. That was my first experience working out in the field after I married.

The hardest work we did was thinning beets. You were required to use a short-handled hoe. The cutting edge is about seven- to eight-inches wide, and the handle is about a foot long. You have to be bent over with the hoe in one hand. You walk down the rows stooped over. You have to work hard, fast, as fast as you can because you were paid by the row, not by the hour. I learned how to do it without straining my back too much. I put my hand on my left knee, and I got so good at it that I'd leave one beet on each stroke. You're supposed to pull one off with your hand if you leave two. I'd go as fast as I could and I'd always leave one and one. Most of them would be chopping, and then picking and separating with two hands. But I was walking backward and going fast. But when I wanted to stand up, I'd have to go very slow and I couldn't stand up straight. I still have a bad back, and I think I got it from the short-handled hoe.

I also used a short-handled hoe in the lettuce fields. The lettuce grows in a bed. You work in little furrows between two rows. First you thin them with the hoe, then you pick off the tops. My brothers-in-law and Arnold and I and some other friends worked there picking the tops off the lettuce. By the time they had taken up one row, I had taken up two. The men would go between the two beds and take one row and break the little balls off. But I took two rows at a time, one with each hand. By the time I finished my two rows at the other end, it was close to a mile long, and my brother-in-law had only taken one row part-way. He said, "I'm quitting! If Jessie can beat me at this kind of work, I'm no good at it." So he never came back. About three or four other men wouldn't go back to work because they were beaten by a woman. They said, "I'm ashamed to have a woman even older than I am work faster than I can. This is women's job." I said, "Hey! What do you mean? You mean the men's job is washing dishes and baking tortillas?" They said working out in the fields is women's work because we were faster at it!

Out in the fields there were never any restrooms. We had to go eight or ten hours without relief. If there wasn't brush or a little ditch, we were forced to wait until we got home! Just the women. The men didn't need to pull their clothes down. Later, when I worked for the Farmworkers, in a hearing I said, "I was working for Russell Giffen, the biggest grower in Huron. These big growers have a lot of money because we earned all that money for them. Because of our sweat and our labor that we put on the land. What they do instead of supplying restrooms and clean water where we can wash our hands, is put posts on the ground with a piece of gunny sack wound around them." That's where we went. And that thing was moved along with us. It was just four stakes stuck in the ground, and then there was canvas or a piece of gunny sack around it. You would be working, and this restroom would be right there. The canvas didn't come up high enough in front for privacy. We made it a practice to go two at a time. One would stand outdoors and watch outside that nobody came along. And then the other would do the same for the one inside. Then we'd go back to work.

La Causa

GROWING UP, I COULD SEE ALL THE INJUSTICES AND I would think, "If only I could do something about it! If only there was somebody who could do something about it!" That was always in the back of my mind. And after I was married, I cared about what was going on, but I felt I couldn't do anything. So I went to work, and I came home to clean the house, and I fixed the food for the next day, took care of the children and the next day went back to work. The whole thing over and over again. Politics to me was something foreign, something I didn't know about. I didn't even listen to the news. I didn't read the newspapers hardly at all. *True Romance* was my thing!

But then late one night in 1962, there was a knock at the door and there were three men. One of them was Cesar Chavez. And the next thing I knew, they were sitting around our table talking about a union. I made coffee. Arnold had already told me about a union for the farmworkers. He was attending their meetings in Fresno, but I didn't. I'd either stay home or stay outside in the car. But then Cesar said, "The women have to be involved. They're the ones working out in the fields with their husbands. If you can take the women out to the fields, you can certainly take them to meetings." So I sat up straight and said to myself, "*That's* what I want!"

When I became involved with the union, I felt I had to get other women involved. Women have been behind men all the time, always. Just waiting to see what the men decide to do, and tell us what to do. In my sister-in-law and brother-in-law's families, the women do a lot of shouting and cussing and they get slapped around. But that's not standing up for what you believe in. It's just trying to boss and not knowing how. I'd hear them scolding their kids and fighting their husbands and I'd say, "Gosh! Why don't you go after the people that have you living like this? Why don't you go after the growers that have you tired from working out in the fields at low wages and keep us poor all the time? Let's go after them! *They're* the cause of our misery!" Then I would say we had to take a part in the things going on around us. "Women can no longer be taken for granted—that we're just going to stay home and do the cooking and cleaning. It's way past the time when our husbands could say, 'You stay home! You have to take care of the children! You have to do as I say!'"

Then some women I spoke to started attending the union meetings, and later they were out on the picket lines.

I think I was made an organizer because in the first place I could relate to the farmworkers, being a lifelong farmworker. I was well-known in the small towns around Fresno. Wherever I went to speak to them, they listened. I told them about how we were excluded from the NLRB in 1935, how we had no benefits, no minimum wage, nothing out in the fields—no restrooms, nothing.[1] I would talk about how we were paid what the grower wanted to pay us, and how we couldn't set a price on our work. I explained that we could do something about these things by joining a union, by working together. I'd ask people how they felt about these many years they had been working out in the fields, how they had been treated. And then we'd all talk about it. They would say, "I was working for so-and-so, and when I complained about something that happened there, I was fired." I said, "Well! Do you think we should be putting up with this in this modern age? You know, we're not back in the twenties. We can stand up! We can talk back! It's not like when I was a little kid and my grandmother used to say, 'You have to especially respect the Anglos,' 'Yessir,' 'Yes, Ma'am!' That's over. This country is very rich, and we want a share of the money these growers make of our sweat and our work by exploiting us and our children!" I'd have my sign-up book and I'd say, "If anyone wants to become a member of the union, I can make you a member right now." And they'd agree!

So I found out that I could organize them and make members of them. Then I offered to help them, like taking them to the doctor's and translating for them, filling out papers that they needed to fill out, writing their letters for those that couldn't write. A lot of people confided in me. Through the letter-writing, I knew a lot of the problems they were having back home, and they knew they could trust me, that I wouldn't tell anyone else about what I had written or read. So that's why they came to me.

There was a migrant camp in Parlier. And these people, the migrants, were being used as strikebreakers. I had something to do with building that camp. By that time, I had been put on the board of the Fresno County Economic Opportunity Commission, and I was supporting migrant housing for farmworkers. But I had no idea it was going to be turned almost into a concentration camp or prison. The houses were just like matchboxes—square, a room for living, a room for cooking, a bathroom that didn't have a door, just a curtain. The houses are so close together that if one catches fire, the next one does, too, and children have burned in them. It happened in Parlier.

So I went to the camp office and said I wanted to go in and visit. By this time, I was well-known as a radical, an educator, and a troublemaker! The man in the office asked what I wanted to talk about. I just wanted to visit, I said.

"Well, you have to sign your name here." I said, "I also would like to know when I can use the hall for a meeting."

"What kind of meeting?"

"An organizing meeting." You see, when it was built, they told us there was supposed to be a hall built for parties and whatever. I felt we could use it for a meeting to talk to the people. But he said, "We can't authorize you to come in here and talk to the people about a union, but you can write Governor Reagan and ask for permission."[2] I left.

I met a nurse who had to go to this camp. She said,

"Why don't you come with me as my translator?" Even though she spoke perfect Spanish! So both of us went in, and she said she was from the Health Department and I was her translator. I got in there and talked to the people and told them about our union meetings, and at our next meeting they were there. I had to do things like that in order to organize.

It was very hard being a woman organizer. Many of our people my age and older were raised with the old customs in Mexico: where the husband rules, he is king of his house. The wife obeys, and the children, too. So when we first started it was very, very hard. Men gave us the most trouble—neighbors there in Parlier! They were for the union, but they were not taking orders from women, they said. When they formed the ranch committee at Christian Brothers—that's a big wine company, part of it is in Parlier—the ranch committee was all men.[3] We were working under our first contract in Fresno County. The ranch committee had to enforce the contract. If there are any grievances they meet with us and the supervisors. But there were no women on the first committee.

That year, we'd have a union meeting every week. Men, women, and children would come. Women would ask questions and the men would just stand back. I guess they'd say to themselves, "I'll wait for someone to say something before I do." The women were more aggressive than the men. And I'd get up and say, "Let's go on, let's do it!"

When the first contract was up, we talked about there being no women on the ranch committee. I suggested they be on it, and the men went along with this. And so women were elected.

The women took the lead for picketing, and we would talk to the people. It got to the point that we would have to find them, because the men just wouldn't go and they wouldn't take their wives. So we would say, "We're having our picket line at the Safeway in Fresno, and those that don't show up are going to have to pay a five-dollar fine." We couldn't have four or five come to a picket line and have the rest stay home and watch TV. In the end, we had everybody out there.[4]

One time we were picketing—I think it was the early part of 1972—White River Farms in Delano, for a new contract. To go picket, we had to get up early. See, a lot of these growers were chartering buses, and at four or five o'clock in the morning they'd pick up the scabs. So we would follow these labor bosses who chartered the buses.

At White River Farms one morning very early, we were out there by the hundreds by the road, and these people got down and started working out there in the grapes. We were asking them not to work, telling them that there was a strike going on. The grower had two guards at the entrance, and there was a helicopter above us. At other White River Farm ranches they had the sheriff, the county police, *everybody*. But there were pickets at three different ranches, and where we were picketing there wasn't anybody except these two guards. So I said, "Hey! What about the women getting together and let's rush 'em!" And they said, "Do you think we could do that?" And I said, "Of course we can! Let's go in there. Let's get 'em out of there any way we can." So about fifty of us rushed. We went under the vines. We had our banners, and you could see them bobbing up and down, up and down, and we'd go under those rows on our knees and roll over. When the scabs saw us coming they took off. All of them went and they got on the bus. The guards had guns that they would shoot, and something black like smoke or teargas would come out. That scared us, but we still kept on. After we saw all those workers get back on the buses, we went back. Instead of running this time, we rolled over and over all the way out. The vines are about four feet tall, and they have wire where you string up the vines. So you can't walk or run across one of these fences. You have to keep going under these wires. So I tripped, and rolled down about three or four rows before I got up. I rolled so they wouldn't get at me when they were shooting. When I got out there on the road they were getting these big, hard dirty clods and throwing them at us. And then the pickets started doing the same thing. When the first police car came, somebody broke the windshield. We don't know if it was the scabs or someone on the picket lines, but the picketers were blamed.

When we women ran into the fields, we knew we'd be arrested if they caught us. But we went in and we told the scabs, "If you're not coming out we're gonna pull you out!" Later I told Arnold, "See? See what women can do? We got all those men out there to come out!"

At another place, in Kern County, we were sprayed with pesticides. They would come out there with their sprayers and spray us on the picket lines. They have these big tanks that are pulled by a tractor with hoses attached, and they spray the trees with this. They are strong like a water hose, but wider. They get it started and spray the vines and the trees. When we were picketing, they came out there to spray the pickets. What could we do? We tried to get as far away as we could, and then we would come back.

They had goons with these big police dogs on leashes. I think they were trying to scare us by letting them loose on us. But those dogs were whining and straining to get loose because they were scared of all the shouting that we were doing! They weren't very brave! We would shout, "Let them go so they can hide! Why put them through this?"

The next year, in '73, we were picketing another ranch in Coachella. That's the first time I saw any of the Teamsters. They were huge. And they had huge rings on their fingers, making gestures at us, and they had clubs. They started singing God Bless America, because they were super-Americans and we were not. They had these big American flags on the backs of their tee-shirts. They said we were nothing, only Chicanos. All we were asking for was recognition of our union. They had dogs. Oh! They were dirty-mouthed people. When the growers realized how strong we were getting and how we had so many members, when our contracts were up for renewal they called the Teamsters in. And even before we bargained for our new contract, the growers signed up with the Teamsters. Then they claimed they already had a union and couldn't recognize ours. That was another way they had of not signing with UFW. They were signing hundreds of what we called "sweetheart contracts."

Another thing the growers did to break our strikes was to bring in "illegal aliens." I would get a list of names of the scabs and give them to the border patrol. At that time, you see, we were pitted against each other, us and the people from Mexico, so it was either us or them. When I went to the border patrol office, I'd go in and say, "Can I come in?" They'd say, "You can't come in. This is a very small office." They kept telling us they were short of men. But every time I went there, there were all of them with their feet up on the desks in their air-conditioned office. They told me they were under orders not to interfere with labor disputes. So I called Bernie Sisk's office and talked to them about it.[5] Then I came home and called a lot of students who'd been helping us, and other people, and the next morning, there we were at the border patrol. I said, "We're paying our tax money, but not for you to sit here while the illegal aliens are being used to break our strike."

But as I said, we, the strikers, and the illegal aliens were being pitted against each other. And at a hearing in 1973, I told the congressmen, "Our grandparents were illegal aliens once. We've never been against them. We feed them. But you, and you, and you," I pointed at the congressmen, "You Anglos, none of you have more right than these Mexican people here. This land was once Mexico. You came along and built a big fence and said, 'You keep on your side of the fence and we'll keep on ours.' But you came along and got the *braceros* to use them.[6] So it's a problem *you* created. They're our blood brothers and blood sisters and you're using them against us!"

While I was working for the union, I learned about negotiating for a contract. In 1966, when we were negotiating for a contract with Christian Brothers, Dolores Huerta asked me along.[7] "I want you to learn this because eventually you might have to take over the negotiating of the contracts." I'd sit there at those meetings with the Christian Brothers, who were Catholic priests. Dolores and the ranch committee would argue, "You can't say we're asking for too much money, because just think, you have over fifty varieties of fine grapes that go into making the most expensive wines for the church and they sell at very high prices. So why can't these workers share some of the money that comes out of those grapes that they've harvested?" They would bargain back and forth this way. Then the ranch committee would caucus—we would walk out of that meeting room, and we'd drink water and discuss what we were going to say when we went back. We'd say, "They have to meet our demands." We were asking for protective clothing; that they supply the pans we picked the grapes in. We also asked for a smoke device for the tractors. We were on our knees working beside the tractors and we would feel dizzy, smelling all of the smoke from the exhaust pipe for hours. We also didn't have any water on the tractors. To get water we had to go with the tractor driver to where the water was, and then we'd lose time picking and lose money. We demanded that they supply each crew with a can of drinking water, so we could drink water right there when we were thirsty.

Our demands were met, but it was hard bargaining. At one point, one of the Christian Brothers' lawyers said, "Well, sister, it sounds to me like you're asking for the moon for these people." Dolores came back, "Brother, I'm not asking for the moon for the farmworkers. All we want is just a little ray of sunshine for them!" Oh, that sounded beautiful!

In '68, while we were in Parlier, I was put in charge of the hiring hall. My house was right next to the office, and I had an extension to the office phone in my house. I could do the housework and take care of the children, but I could take care of the office, too. Before the contract, the hiring hall was just a union office, where people came to learn about the union. When they got the first contracts, we began dispatching people out to work.

It was up to me to get all the membership cards in order alphabetically. When the grower came to us to ask for workers, I'd look for the ones who were in the union longest, and also working under the Christian Brothers contract. I'd call them: "Can you be ready Monday or Wednesday morning? Be there on time, because you're going to start working for Christian Brothers." One of the things we had to explain over and over to people who had been working for a ranch many years was that no one was going to take their jobs away. The growers told them, "If you sign up for Chavez's union we'll fire you." But the union contract guarantees that the people working here have the right to stay here, so we always made a list of names of people who were working at the ranch. And when the union organizes them, they have the highest seniority, they're the first ones hired.

The hiring hall was also a place where people could meet and talk. A lot of people were migrants who needed to get to know each other. The people who were there all the time were against the migrants. I said, "We have to get these people together. We can't be divided." I was at the hall all day. People would drop by and I'd introduce them.

The second year we had a contract I started working for Christian Brothers. The men were doing the pruning on the grape vines. After they did the pruning, the women's crew would come and tie the vines—that was something we got changed. We made them give pruning jobs to women.

I was made a steward on the women's crew.[8] If there were any grievances, it was up to me to listen and then enforce the contract. For example, the first time we were paid when I started working, during the break the supervisor would come out there with our checks. It was our fifteen-minute break, which the contract gave us the right to. He always came then! We had to walk to the other end of the row, it took us about five minutes to get there, the rest of the fifteen to get our checks, and walk back, and we'd start working. This happened twice. The third time I said, "We're not going to go after our checks this time. They always come during our break and we don't get to rest." So when we saw the pickup coming with the men who had the checks I said, "Nobody move. You just sit here." I walked over to the pickup. I said to the man inside, "Mr. Rager, these women refuse to come out here on their break time. It's their time to rest. So we're asking you, if you must come during our rest period, you take the checks to these ladies." From that day on, every payday he would come to us. That was the sort of thing you had to do to enforce the contract.

I became involved in many of the activities in the community—school board meetings, city council meetings, everything that I could get into. For example, I began fighting for bilingual education in Parlier, went to a lot of meetings about it and spoke about it.

You see, when I was a nine-year-old child going to school, I couldn't speak English. I remember vividly one day all the children, mostly Chicanos, were lined up, and we had to stand before this lady all dressed in white, a health nurse. She told me to open my mouth and I just stared at her. She stuck a stick to push my tongue down, and I couldn't help it: I vomited all over her dress. Oh! I started crying, and the teacher came up and she kept saying, "I'm sorry. I'm sorry." Those words stuck to me; I even dreamed them.

Another time something else happened when I ran out of underwear! See, we were very poor, and when I ran out of underwear, grandmother tore open a pillow and used the red satin to make some drawers for me. I was ashamed; I didn't want nobody to see me. I was dressed very different from all the other children in the first place. My dresses were almost down to my ankles and they were gathered in the waist with a drawstring that my grandmother made me, and high boy's shoes and heavy black stockings.

When I got the red underwear, I was out there after school like a little monkey up on the swings and two

Anglo girls about my age started teasing me: "Oh, she's got red panties! red panties!" and they tried to lift my dress up. By this time, I was off the swings and standing against the wall. When one of the older girls leaned over to pull my dress up, I lifted my knee and hit her nose and she started bleeding and crying. The teacher came over and she slapped me. But since I didn't know English, I couldn't tell her, I couldn't explain what had happened.

To top it off, being a migrant worker I changed schools about every three to four weeks. As soon as one crop was picked, we went on to the next one. I'd go to school for about a week or two, then I was transferred. Every time we transferred I had a pain in my stomach, I was shaking, scared to go to school.

This is why I began fighting for bilingual education. I didn't want what happened to me to happen to the little children in Parlier whose parents couldn't speak English.

Parlier is over eighty-five percent Chicano, yet during that time there were no Chicanos on the school board, on the police force, nowhere. Now it's changed; we fought to get a Chicano mayor and officials. But then I was asking people, "Why are we always asked to go to the public school for our meetings? Why can't they come over to our side of town in Parlier?" So we began having meetings in *la colonia*[9] at the Headstart Center, and there we pushed for bilingual education.

Fresno County didn't give food stamps to the people—only surplus food.[10] There were no vegetables, no meat, just staples like whole powdered milk, cheese, butter. At the migrant camp in Parlier, the people were there a month and a half before work started, and since they'd borrowed money to get to California, they didn't have any food. I'd drive them into Fresno to the welfare department and translate for them, and they'd get food, but half of it they didn't eat. We heard about other counties where they had food stamps to go to the store and buy meat and milk and fresh vegetables for the children. So we began talking about getting that in Fresno. Finally, we had Senate hearings at the Convention Center in Fresno. There were hundreds of people listening. A man I know comes to me and says, "Jessie, you're next." He'd been going to speak, but he said he wanted me to speak in his place. I started in Spanish, and the senators were looking at each other, you know, saying, "What's going on?" So then I said, "Now, for the benefit of those who can't speak Spanish, I'll translate. They tell us there's no money for food stamps for poor people. But if there is money enough to fight a war in Vietnam, and if there is money enough for Governor Reagan's wife to buy a three-thousand-dollar dress for the Inauguration Ball, there should be money enough to feed these people. The nutrition experts say surplus food is full of vitamins. I've taken a look at that food, this cornmeal, and I've seen them come up and down. But you know, we don't call them vitamins, we call them weevils!" Everybody began laughing and whistling and shouting. In the end, we finally got food stamps for the people in Fresno County.

Sometimes I'd just stop to think: what if our parents had done what we were doing now? My grandparents were poor. They were humble. They never learned to speak English. They felt God meant them to be poor. It was against their religion to fight. I remember there was a huge policeman named Marcos, when I was a child, who used to go around on a horse. My grandmother would say, "Here comes Marcos," and we just grew up thinking, "He's law and order." But during the strikes I stood up to them. They'd come up to arrest me and I'd say, "O.K., here I come if you want. Arrest me!"

Notes

1 The National Labor Relations Board (NLRB) was established by President Franklin Delano Roosevelt in 1933. Its purpose was to settle differences between employers and employees. The board was set up under the National Labor Relations Act, which made union negotiations between employers and employees legal for the first time in the United States. The act, and the board set up to implement it, were historical landmarks in the history of unionism. But two major groups of workers were excluded by the act and its board—domestic workers (who were mostly women) and farmworkers (who were mainly Chicanos, Filipinos, and blacks). Both major groups were among the poorest of the United States working class.

2 Reagan was the Republican governor of California. A conservative, he was known to be unfriendly to the United Farmworkers.

3 On every farm, the union created a ranch committee elected by the workers. The committee is the grassroots base of the union. If you have an on-the-job complaint, you bring it to the ranch committee, which then discusses the complaint with the supervisor. Before the ranch committee was introduced by the union, individual workers had to get up nerve to complain about abuses on their own—and often they were fired on the spot when they dared speak up. The ranch committee put the union behind them and gave them a democratically-elected group for support.

4 The picket lines at the Safeway chain were set up to keep consumers from shopping at a store that sold nonunion grapes. The picket lines at the ranches were set up to keep workers from working.

5 Sisk was a Democratic congressman with a reputation of sympathy for farmworkers and small farmers. Later, Sisk turned out far more sympathetic to the big growers.

6 Under a program begun in World War II, *braceros* ("hired hands," from the Spanish word, *brazo*, arm), were brought in by the growers to feed their labor needs. The *braceros* were ill-treated and badly paid.

7 Dolores Huerta, one of the founders of the union, has held key leadership positions in the UFW.

8 Every union has its workers elect "shop stewards" from their midst. These officially-elected union representatives remain on the job, working side-by-side with the other employees. Their responsibility is to provide information to their co-workers about the union, and to deal with any complaints—"grievances"—workers may have. The steward is empowered to go to the manager or boss on the workers' behalf, and to consult with other union officials about on-the-job problems.

9 The Chicano neighborhood.

10 In 1964, Congress established a program under which low-income people could "pay" for food at stores by using stamps issued by the government. Your eligibility for food stamps depended on your income. When the Welfare office sent you surplus food, you had to eat what you got: you had no choice. But you could take food stamps to your local store, and buy what you wanted.

Deferred

Langston Hughes

This year, maybe, do you think I can graduate?
I'm already two years late.
Dropped out six months when I was seven,
a year when I was eleven,
then got put back when we came North.
To get through high school at twenty's kind of late—
But maybe this year I can graduate.

Maybe now I can have that white enamel stove
I dreamed about when we first fell in love
eighteen years ago.
But you know,
rooming and everything
then kids,
cold-water flat and all that.
But now my daughter's married
And my boy's most grown—
quit school to work—
and where we're moving
there ain't no stove—
Maybe I can buy that white enamel stove!

From Montage of a Dream Deferred *by Langston Hughes. Copyright © 1951 by Langston Hughes. Copyright renewed 1979 by George Houston Bass. Reprinted by permission of Harold Ober Associates Inc.*

Me, I always did want to study French.
It don't make sense—
I'll never go to France,
but night schools teach French.
Now at last I've got a job
where I get off at five,
in time to wash and dress,
so, s'il-vous plait, I'll study French!
Someday,
I'm gonna buy two new suits
at once!

All I want is
one more bottle of gin.

All I want is to see
my furniture paid for.

All I want is a wife who will
work with me and not against me. Say,
baby, could you see your way clear?

Heaven, heaven, is my home!
This world I'll leave behind.
When I set my feet in glory
I'll have a throne for mine!

I want to pass the civil service.

I want a television set.

Deferred

You know, as old as I am,
I ain't never
owned a decent radio yet?

I'd like to take up Bach.

    Montage
    of a dream
    deferred.

Buddy, have you heard?

Fast Car

Tracy Chapman

You got a fast car
I want a ticket to anywhere
Maybe we can make a deal
Maybe together we can get somewhere

Anyplace is better
Starting from zero got nothing to lose
Maybe we'll make something
But me myself I got nothing to prove

You got a fast car
And I got a plan to get us out of here
I been working at the convenience store
Managed to save just a little bit of money
We won't have to drive too far
Just 'cross the border and into the city
You and I can both get jobs
And finally see what it means to be living

"Fast Car" by Tracy Chapman. Copyright © 1988 by EMI April Music Inc. and Purple Rabbit Music. All Rights Controlled and Administered by EMI April Music Inc. All Rights Reserved. International Copyright Secured. Used by permission.

You see my old man's got a problem
He live with the bottle that's the way it is
He says his body's too old for working
I say his body's too young to look like his
My mama went off and left him
She wanted more from life than he could give
I said somebody's got to take care of him
So I quit school and that's what I did

You got a fast car
But is it fast enough so we can fly away
We gotta make a decision
We leave tonight or live and die this way

I remember we were driving driving in your car
The speed so fast I felt like I was drunk
City lights lay out before us
And your arm felt nice wrapped 'round my shoulder
And I had a feeling that I belonged
And I had a feeling I could be someone, be someone, be someone

You got a fast car
And we go cruising to entertain ourselves
You still ain't got a job
And I work in a market as a checkout girl
I know things will get better
You'll find work and I'll get promoted
We'll move out of the shelter
Buy a big house and live in the suburbs

I remember we were driving driving in your car
The speed so fast I felt like I was drunk
City lights lay out before us
And your arm felt nice wrapped 'round my shoulder
And I had a feeling that I belonged
And I had a feeling that I could be someone, be someone, be someone

You got a fast car
And I got a job that pays all our bills
You stay out drinking late at the bar
See more of your friends than you do of your kids
I'd always hoped for better
Thought maybe together you and me would find it
I got no plans I ain't going nowhere
So take your fast car and keep on driving

I remember we were driving driving in your car
The speed so fast I felt like I was drunk
City lights lay out before us
And your arm felt nice wrapped 'round my shoulder
And I had a feeling that I belonged
And I had a feeling that I could be someone, be someone, be someone

You got a fast car
But is it fast enough so you can fly away
You gotta make a decision
You leave tonight or live and die this way.

Just a Housewife

Jesusita Novarro
edited by Studs Terkel

I START MY DAY HERE AT FIVE O'CLOCK. I GET UP and prepare all the children's clothes. If there's shoes to shine, I do it in the morning. About seven o'clock I bathe the children. I leave my baby with the baby sitter and I go to work at the settlement house. I work until twelve o'clock. Sometimes I'll work longer if I have to go to welfare and get a check for somebody. When I get back, I try to make hot food for the kids to eat. In the afternoon it's pretty well on my own. I scrub and clean and cook and do whatever I have to do.

Welfare makes you feel like you're nothing. Like you're laying back and not doing anything and it's falling in your lap. But you must understand, mothers,

From Working People Talk About What They Do All Day and How They Feel About What They Do *by Studs Terkel. Copyright © 1972, 1974 by Studs Terkel. Reprinted by permission of Pantheon Books, a division of Random House, Inc.*

too, work. My house is clean. I've been scrubbing since this morning. You could check my clothes, all washed and ironed. I'm home and I'm working. I am a working mother.

A job that a woman in a house is doing is a tedious job—especially if you want to do it right. If you do it slipshod, then it's not so bad. I'm pretty much of a perfectionist. I tell my kids, hang a towel. I don't want it thrown away. That is very hard. It's a constant game of picking up this, picking up that. And putting this away, so the house'll be clean.

Some men work eight hours a day. There are mothers that work eleven, twelve hours a day. We get up at night, a baby vomits, you have to be calling the doctor, you have to be changing the baby. When do you get a break, really? You don't. This is an all-around job, day and night. Why do they say it's charity? We're working for our money. I am working for this check. It is not charity. We are giving some kind of home to these children.

I'm so busy all day I don't have time to daydream. I pray a lot. I pray to God to give me strength. If He should take a child away from me, to have the strength to accept it. It's His kid. He just borrowed him to me.

I used to get in and close the door. Now I speak up for my right. I walk with my head up. If I want to wear big earrings, I do. If I'm overweight, that's too bad. I've gotten completely over feeling where I'm little. I'm working now, I'm pulling my weight. I'm gonna get off welfare in time, that's my goal—get off.

It's living off welfare and feeling that you're taking something for nothing the way people have said. You get to think maybe you are. You get to think, Why am I so stupid? Why can't I work? Why do I have to live this way? It's not enough to live on anyway. You feel degraded.

The other day I was at the hospital and I went to pay my bill. This nurse came and gave me the green card. Green card is for welfare. She went right in front of me and gave it to the cashier. She said, "I wish I could stay home and let the money fall in my lap." I felt rotten. I was just burning inside. You hear this all the way around you. The doctor doesn't even look at you. People are ashamed to show that green card. Why can't a woman just get a check in the mail: Here, this check is for you. Forget welfare. You're a mother who works.

This nurse, to her way of thinking, she represents the working people. The ones with the green card, we represent the lazy no-goods. This is what she was saying. They're the good ones and we're the bad guys.

You know what happened at the hospital? I was put in a nice room, semiprivate. You stay there until someone with insurance comes in and then you get pushed up to the fifth floor. There's about six people in there, and nobody comes even if you ring. I said, "Listen lady, you can put me on the roof. You just find out what's the matter with me so I can get the hell out of here."

How are you going to get people off welfare if they're constantly being pushed down? If they're constantly feeling they're not good for anything? People say, I'm down, I'll stay down. And this goes on generation to generation to generation. Their daughter and their daughter and their daughter. So how do you break this up? These kids don't ask to be born—these kids are gonna grow up and give their lives one day. There will always be a Vietnam.

There will always be war. There always has been. The way the world is run, yes, there will always be war. Why? I really don't know. Nobody has ever told me. I was so busy handling my own affairs and taking care of my children and trying to make my own money and calling up welfare when my checks are late or something has been stolen. All I know is what's going on here. I'm an intelligent woman up to a certain point, and after that... I wish I knew. I guess the big shots decided the war. I don't question it, because I've been busy fighting my own little war for so long.

The head of the settlement house wants me to take the social worker's job when I get back to work. I visit homes, I talk to mothers. I try to make them aware that they got something to give. I don't try to work out the problems. This is no good. I try to help them come to some kind of a decision. If there's no decision, to live with it, because some problem doesn't have any answer.

There was one mother that needed shoes, I found shoes for her. There was another mother that needed money because her check was late. I found someplace for her to borrow a couple of dollars. It's like a fund. I could borrow a couple of dollars until my check comes, then when my check comes I give it back. How much time have mothers left to go out and do this? How many of us have given time so other mothers could learn to speak English, so they'll be able to go to work. We do it gladly because the Lord gave us English.

I went to one woman's house and she's Spanish speaking. I was talking to her in English and she wouldn't unbend. I could see the fear in her eyes. So I started talking Spanish. Right away, she invited me for coffee and she was telling me the latest news...

I would like to help mothers be aware of how they can give to the community. Not the whole day—maybe three, four hours. And get paid for it. There's nothing more proud for you to receive a check where you worked at. It's yours, you done it.

▲▼▲

The people from the settlement house began visiting me, visiting welfare mothers, trying to get them interested in cooking projects and sewing. They began knocking on my door. At the beginning I was angry. It was just like I drew a curtain all around me. I didn't think I was really good for anything. So I kind of drew back. Just kept my troubles to myself, like vegetating. When these people began calling on me, I began to see that I could talk and that I did have a brain. I became a volunteer.

I want to be a social worker. Somebody that is not indifferent, that bends an ear to everybody. You cannot be slobberish. You cannot cry with the people. Even if you cry inside, you must keep a level head. You have to try to help that person get over this bump. I would go into a house and try to make friends. Not as a spy. The ladies have it that welfare comes as spies to see what you have. Or you gotta hide everything 'cause welfare is coming. There is this fear the social worker is gonna holler, because they got something, maybe a man or a boyfriend. I wouldn't take any notes or pens or paper or pencils or anything. I would just go into the house and talk. Of course, I would look around to see what kind of environment it is. This you have to absorb. You wouldn't say it, but you would take it in.

I promised myself if I ever get to work all day, I'm going to buy me a little insurance. So the next time I go to the hospital I'll go to the room I want to go. I'm gonna stay there until it's time for me to leave, because I'm gonna pay my own bill. I don't like to feel rotten. I want my children, when they grow up, they don't have to live on it. I want to learn more. I'm hungry for knowledge. I want to do something. I'm searching for something. I don't know what it is.

Work and Dignity

All work, even cotton-spinning, is noble; work is alone noble...A life of ease is not for any man, nor for any god.

Thomas Carlyle

Honor lies in honest toil.

Grover Cleveland

There is no substitute for hard work.

Thomas Edison, interview on Prohibition

Thank God every morning when you get up that you have something to do that day which must be done, whether you like it or not. Being forced to work, and forced to do your best, will breed in you temperance and self-control, diligence and strength of will, cheerfulness and content, and a hundred other virtues which the idle never know.

Charles Kingsley, letter

The sum of wisdom is that the time is never lost that is devoted to work.

Ralph Waldo Emerson, Society & Solitude: Success

The idle man does not know what it is to enjoy rest. Hard work, moreover, not only tends to give us rest for the body, but, what is even more important, peace to the mind.

Sir John Lubbock, The Pleasures of Life

The white man works like a slave all his life in order to retire, to be able to loaf and hunt and fish. We already have this for which the white man is working. So why should we adopt his ways and work all our life for what we already have.

Sioux Indian,
from The New Indians *by Stan Steiner*

It is work which gives flavor to life.

Amiel, journal, 3-21-1881

Work is something you want to get done; play is something you just like doing.

Harry Leon Wilson, The Spenders

My young men shall never work. Men who work cannot dream, and wisdom comes in dreams.

You ask me to plow the ground. Shall I take a knife and tear my mother's breast? Then when I die she will not take me to her bosom to rest.

You ask me to dig for stone. Shall I dig under her skin for bones? Then when I die I cannot enter her body to be born again.

You ask me to cut grass and make hay and sell it and be rich like white men. But how dare I cut my mother's hair?

It is a bad law, and my people cannot obey it. I want my people to stay with me here. All the dead men will come to life again. We must wait here in the house of our fathers and be ready to meet them in the body of our mother.

Smohalla, a Nez Perce Indian

I like work; it fascinates me. I can sit and look at it for hours.

Jerome K. Jerome, Three Men in a Boat

If any would not work, neither should he eat.

2 Thess. 3:10.

Work is love made visible. And if you cannot work with love but only with distaste, it is better that you should leave your work and sit at the gate of the temple and take alms of those who work with joy.

> *Kahlil Gibran,* The Prophet

Do all your work as though you had a thousand years to live, and as you would if you knew you must die tomorrow.

> *Mother Ann Lee, from* A Collection of Shaker Thoughts
> *by Colin Becket Richmond*

Work, Status, and Recognition

"A fair day's-wages for a fair day's work": it is as just a demand as governed men ever made of governing. It is the everlasting right of man.

Thomas Carlyle

The president keeps repeating the "dignity of work" idea. What dignity? Wages are the measure of dignity that society puts on a job. Wages and nothing else. There is no dignity in starvation. Nobody denies, least of all poor women, that there is dignity and satisfaction in being able to support your kids through honest labor.

We wish we could do it.

If I were president, I would solve this so-called welfare crisis in a minute and go a long way toward liberating every woman. I'd just issue a proclamation that "woman's" work is *real* work.

In other words, I'd start paying women a living wage for doing the work we are already doing—childraising and housekeeping. And the welfare crisis would be over, just like that.

Johnnie Tillmon, welfare mother
from "Welfare Is a Women's Issue,"
in America's Working Women

Man may work from sun to sun,
But woman's work is never done.

Anonymous

It's not just the work. Somebody built the pyramids. Somebody's going to build something. Pyramids. Empire State Building—these things just don't happen. There's hard work behind it. I would like to see a building, say, the Empire State. I would like to see on one side of it a foot-wide strip from top to bottom with the name of every bricklayer, the name of every electrician, with all the names. So when a guy walked by, he could take his son and say, "See, that's me over there on the forty-fifth floor. I put the steel beam in." Picasso can point to a painting. What can I point to? A writer can point to a book. Everybody should have something to point to.

It's the not-recognition by other people. To say a woman is *just* a housewife is degrading, right?...It's also degrading to say *just* a laborer.

Mike LeFevre
from Working *by Studs Terkel*

The seed ye sow, another reaps;
The wealth ye find, another keeps;
The robes ye weave, another wears;
The arms ye forge, another bears.

Percy Bysshe Shelley, "Song To the Men of England"

A man said, "Don't you think someone who becomes an auto mechanic and is good at it should also be recognized? He's a specialist, too, like the man who goes to be a doctor." Yet he's not thought of that way. What difference? It's a shame that people aren't looked at as each job being special unto itself. I can't work on a car, yet I see people who can do it beautifully. Like they have such a feel for it. Some people can write books, other people can do marvelous things in other ways...

Nancy Rogers, bank teller
from Working *by Studs Terkel*

Which of us is to do the hard and dirty work for the rest, and for what pay? Who is to do the pleasant and clean work, and for what pay?

John Ruskin, Sesame and Lilies: King's Treasuries

No race can prosper till it learns that there is as much dignity in tilling a field as in writing a book.

Booker T. Washington, Up from Slavery

No man is born into the world whose work is not born with him; there is always work, and tools to work withal, for those who will.

James Russell Lowell, A Glance Behind the Curtain

...we want to do two things in modern society. We want one class of persons to have a liberal education, and we want another class of persons, a very much larger class, of necessity, in every society, to forego the privileges of a liberal education and fit themselves to perform specific difficult manual tasks. You cannot train them for both in the time that you have at your disposal. They must make a selection, and you must make a selection.

Woodrow Wilson
Quoted in Illiterate America *by Jonathan Kozol*

People say, "No one does good work any more." I don't believe it. You know who's saying that? The man at the top, who says the people beneath him are not doing a good job. He's the one who always said, "You're nothing."

Dolores Dante, waitress
from Working *by Studs Terkel*

I don't think anybody's gonna say their work's satisfyin', gratifyin', unless you're in business for yourself. I don't think you're satisfied workin' for the other person.

Bob Sanders, strip miner
from Working *by Studs Terkel*

Work, Status, and Recognition

Upon the sacredness of property civilization itself depends—the right of the laborer to his hundred dollars in the savings bank, and equally the legal right of the millionaire to his millions.

Andrew Carnegie, from Rereading America

The hours are long, the pay is small,
So take your time and buck them all.

IWW Poster

Repetitive labour—the doing of one thing over and over again and always in the same way—is a terrifying prospect to a certain kind of mind. It is terrifying to me. I could not possibly do the same thing day in and day out, but to other minds, perhaps I might say the majority of minds, repetitive operations hold no terrors. In fact, to some types of mind thought is absolutely appalling. To them the ideal job is one where the creative instinct need not be expressed. The jobs where it is necessary to put in mind as well as muscle have very few takers…the average worker I am sorry to say wants a job in which he does not have to put forth much physical exertion—above all, he wants a job in which he does not have to think.

…I have not been able to discover that repetitive labour injures a man in any way.

Henry Ford, My Life and Work

You do it automatically, like a monkey or a dog would do something by conditioning. You feel stagnant; everything is over and over and over. It seems like you're just going to work and your whole purpose in life is to do this operation, and you come home and you're so tired from working the hours, trying to keep up with the (assembly) line, you feel you're not making any advancement whatsoever. This makes the average individual feel sort of like a vegetable.

Autoworker
from Root and Branch

...the work is *external* to the worker...it is not a part of his nature...he does not fulfill himself in his work but denies himself, has a feeling of misery, not of well-being, does not develop freely a physical and mental energy, but is physically exhausted and mentally debased. The worker therefore feels himself at home only during his leisure, whereas at work he feels homeless. His work is not voluntary but imposed, forced labor. It is not the satisfaction of a need, but only a means for satisfying other needs.

Karl Marx, from Selected Writings in Sociology and Social Philosophy, *edited by Tom Bottomore*

Constant labor of one uniform kind destroys the intensity and flow of a man's animal spirits, which find recreation and delight in mere change of activity.

Karl Marx, Capital

Jobs are not big enough for people. It's not just the assembly line worker whose job is too small for his spirit, you know? A job like mine, if you really put your spirit into it, you would sabotage immediately. You don't dare. So you absent your spirit from it. My mind has been so divorced from my job, except as a source of income, it's really absurd...

It's so demeaning to be there and not be challenged. It's humiliation, because I feel I'm being forced into doing something I would never do of my own free will...

When you ask most people who they are, they define themselves by their jobs. "I'm a doctor." "I'm a radio announcer." "I'm a carpenter." If somebody asks me, I say, "I'm Nora Watson."

Nora Watson, editor
from Working *by Studs Terkel*